BEHiND THE SCENES
BiOGRAPHiES

WHAT YOU NEVER KNEW ABOUT

>>> ——————————— <<<

BTS

by Martha E. H. Rustad

CAPSTONE PRESS
a capstone imprint

This is an unauthorized biography.

Published by Spark, an imprint of Capstone
1710 Roe Crest Drive, North Mankato, Minnesota 56003
capstonepub.com

Library of Congress Cataloging-in-Publication Data
Names: Rustad, Martha E. H. (Martha Elizabeth Hillman), 1975- author.
Title: What you never knew about BTS / Martha E. H. Rustad.
Description: North Mankato, Minnesota : Capstone Press, 2022. | Series: Behind the scenes biographies | Includes bibliographical references and index. | Audience: Ages 9-11 | Audience: Grades 4-6 | Summary: "South Korean boyband BTS has taken the music world by storm with their catchy lyrics, smooth style, and killer dance moves. But what happens when they're not singing and dancing? High-interest details and bold photos of this musical supergroup will enthrall reluctant and struggling readers, while carefully leveled text will leave them feeling confident."— Provided by publisher.
Identifiers: LCCN 2022008155 (print) | LCCN 2022008156 (ebook) | ISBN 9781666357004 (hardcover) | ISBN 9781669040095 (paperback) | ISBN 9781666357011 (pdf) | ISBN 9781666357035 (kindle edition)
Subjects: LCSH: BTS (Musical group)—Juvenile literature. | Rock musicians—Korea (South)—Juvenile literature. | Boy bands—Korea (South)—Juvenile literature.
Classification: LCC ML3930.B89 (print) | LCC ML3930.B89 (ebook) | DDC 782.4216/3095195 [B]—dc23
LC record available at https://lccn.loc.gov/2022008155
LC ebook record available at https://lccn.loc.gov/2022008156

Editorial Credits
Editor: Mandy Robbins; Designer: Heidi Thompson; Media Researcher: Jo Miller; Production Specialist: Tori Abraham

Image Credits
Associated Press: Chris Pizzello, 14, 21 (top), zz/John Nacion/STAR MAX/IPx, Cover; Getty Images: Cindy Ord, 9, Lester Cohen, 4, Michael Kovac, 6, The Chosunilbo JNS, 25 (right), VALERIE MACON, 26; Shutterstock: AlexRoz, 24 (right), Dragana Gordic, 17, F8 studio, 25 (left), Featureflash Photo Agency, 18, Jamie Lamor Thompson, 10, Kathy Hutchins, 29, mokokomo, 20, Naumova Ekaterina, 15, 24 (left), nikkytok, 20, phive, 22, Pixel-Shot, 19, Rawpixel.com, 16, Shutterstock Vector, 17, Silvia Elizabeth Pangaro, 12 (all), 13 (all), Sunflowerr, 20, thanakornphoto, 28, yatate, 21

All internet sites appearing in back matter were available and accurate when this book was sent to press.

◇ ◇ ◇ ◇ ◇ ◇ ◇ ◇ ◇ ◇ ◇ ◇ ◇ ◇ ◇ ◇ ◇ ◇ ◇ ◇

TABLE OF CONTENTS

Words in **bold** are in the glossary.

LIVE ON
STAGE!

You're in a dark arena. The lights come up. The music starts. People scream. Here comes BTS!

What does BTS do before their concerts? They repeat "Bangtan!" three times. But do you know what it means? Read on to find out!

FACT

BTS was formed in 2010. RM was the first member.

ARE YOU SMOOTH
LIKE BUTTER?

Are you part of the BTS ARMY?

Time to test your knowledge!

1. What was their first song recorded in English?

2. Which member learned English from watching *Friends*?

3. Who collects Super Mario toys?

4. Who was the president of his high school?

5. Who is a talented painter?

6. Who started out as a dancer?

7. What does ARMY stand for?

1. "Dynamite" **2.** RM **3.** Jin

4. Jimin **5.** Jungkook **6.** J-Hope

7. Adorable Representative M.C. for Youth

Do you know what BTS stands for? In Korean, it is Bangtan Sonyeondan. In English, this means Bulletproof Boy Scouts. That wasn't the first name option. The band was almost named Big Kidz or Young Nation.

FACT

BTS has broken many world records with their music. In 2020, the music video for "Dynamite" was the most-viewed YouTube song in 24 hours!

Most BTS lyrics are in Korean. Many fans want to learn Korean. The band sings in other languages too. The BTS ARMY translates songs into other languages.

Can you name the language BTS hasn't used in a song or video?

- **Sign language**
- **French**
- **Japanese**
- **Spanish**

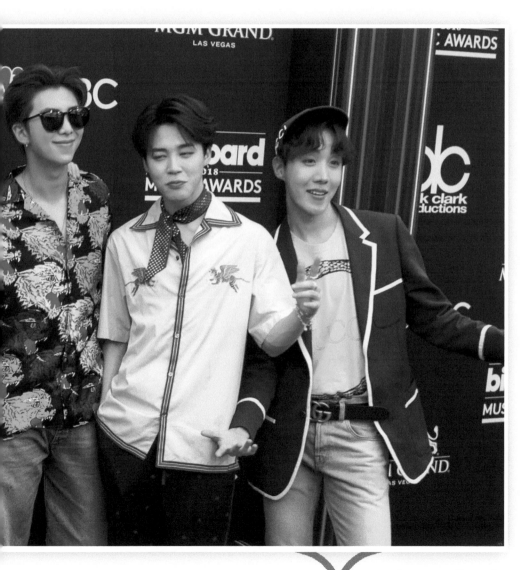

Answer: French

Many of the band members use nicknames. Do you know their real names too?

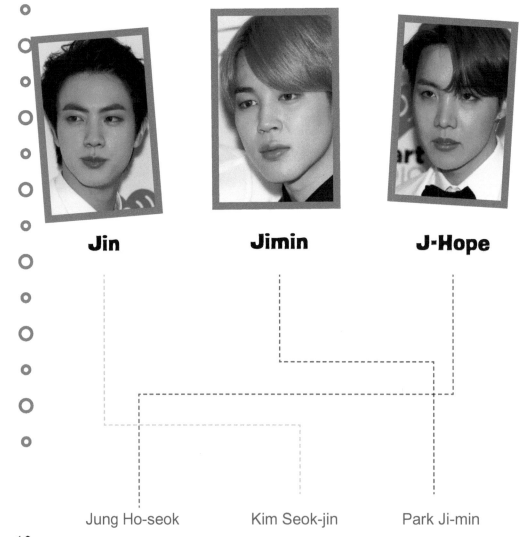

Jin   **Jimin**   **J-Hope**

Jung Ho-seok   Kim Seok-jin   Park Ji-min

The BTS members get along most of the time. How do they settle disagreements? They play rock-paper-scissors!

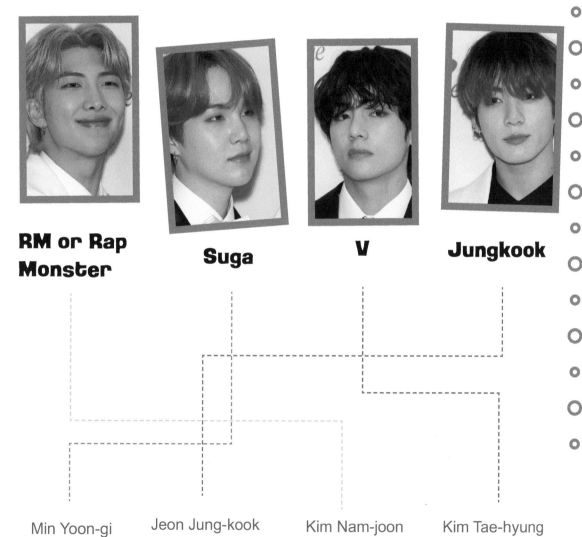

RM or Rap Monster

Suga

V

Jungkook

Min Yoon-gi

Jeon Jung-kook

Kim Nam-joon

Kim Tae-hyung

FANS ARE THEIR
UNIVERSE

BTS always thanks their ARMY. At award shows, they bow to show love for the fans. Jin wrote fans a thank-you note. They even sing about their fans in "We Are Bulletproof."

Fans show their love too. Jimin's fans wrote a song about him.

ARMY members say, "I purple you." It means, "I love and trust you." BTS says it back to fans.

The band's social media numbers are sky-high! They have more than 60 million Instagram followers. An ARMY of 47 million and growing watch their TikTok videos. Over 44 million read their tweets. More than 64 million follow them on YouTube.

COLOR AND
STYLE

BTS uses color to stand out.
Each singer has a different colored
microphone. They love to change their
hair color. The guys like to use makeup
and nail polish too.

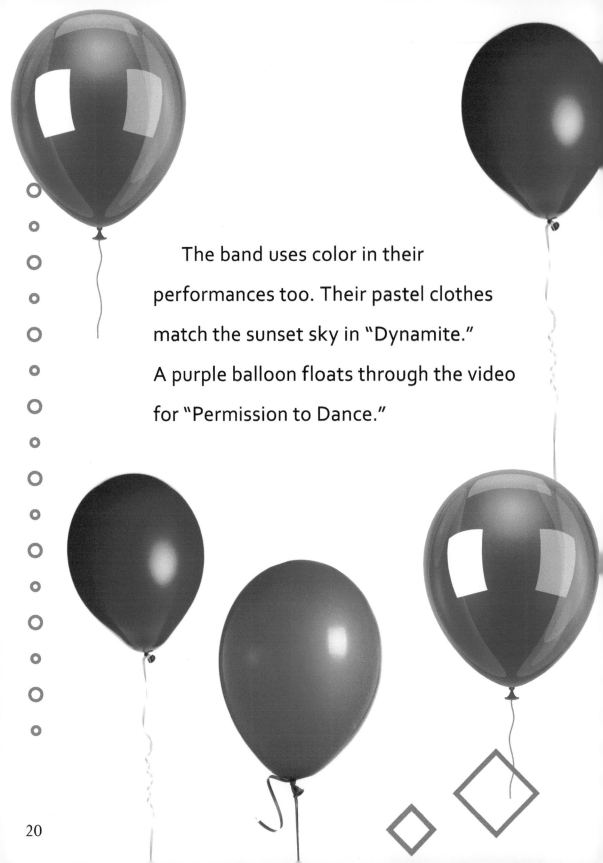

The band uses color in their performances too. Their pastel clothes match the sunset sky in "Dynamite." A purple balloon floats through the video for "Permission to Dance."

BTS took their love of color to the 2021
American Music Awards. They sang "Butter"
in yellow suits on a yellow stage.

HAPPY
BIRTHDAY!

Time for a birthday celebration! The Bangtan Boys read all their online well-wishes. Sometimes they post videos singing to each other too.

Jin races to wish his bandmates happy birthday. He sometimes says it the day before, just to be first.

Imagine getting a gold bar for your birthday! A fan sent that to Jungkook.

Jungkook

Fans planted trees on RM's birthday. Suga got a strawberry cake. Jimin's dad sends him birthday flowers. ARMY put up a billboard to celebrate J-Hope's birthday. On V's birthday, the other guys posted silly photos of him.

Jimin

GIVING
BACK

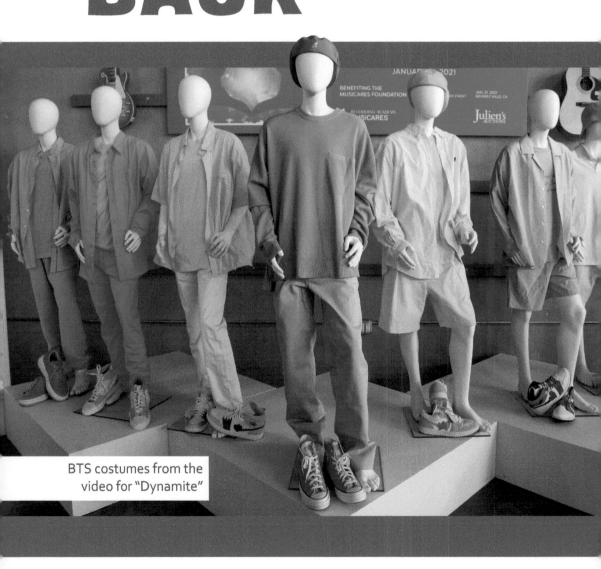

BTS costumes from the
video for "Dynamite"

The members of BTS make big money. They give it back in many ways. They help to feed hungry people. They gave money to help kids with mental health and bullying issues. They **donated** costumes to raise money for COVID-19 relief.

ARMY and BTS work together too. They joined together to raise money for **orphans**, **refugees**, and people hurt by disasters.

BACK **HOME**

Seoul, South Korea

BTS lives in South Korea. They used to all share a small apartment in Seoul. Now they each have their own huge apartment.

Every South Korean male must serve in the **military**. The government might give BTS a pass. Why? They sell millions of records and bring in money for the country. They are also the reason many people around the world are learning the Korean language.

Glossary

donate (DOH-nate)—to give something as a gift to a charity or cause

military (MIL-uh-ter-ee)—the armed forces of a state or country

orphan (OR-fuhn)—a child whose parents have died

refugee (ref-yuh-JEE)—a person who has been forced to leave his or her home to escape war or persecution

Read More

Brown, Helen. *BTS: K-Pop Kings.* San Diego: Printers Row Publishing Group, 2019.

Kawa, Katie. *BTS: Making a Difference as a Band.* New York: KidHaven, 2023.

Schwartz, Heather E. *BTS: K-Pop Fan Favorites.* Minneapolis: Lerner, 2022.

Internet Sites

BTS: Official Site

ibighit.com/bts/eng/profile/

Fan Favorites: BTS

timeforkids.com/g56/fan-favorites-2/?rl=en-890

US BTS ARMY

usbtsarmy.com

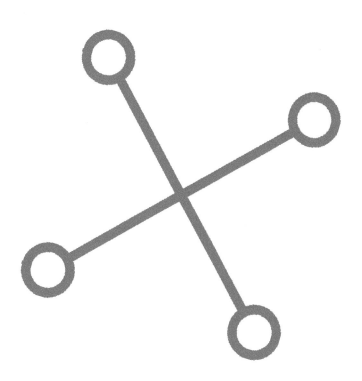

Index

About the Author

Martha E. H. Rustad is the author of more than 300 nonfiction children's books, on topics ranging from baby ducks to black holes to ancient Babylon. She lives with her family in Brainerd, Minnesota.